Aunt Fanny Learns Forestry:
Managing Timberland as an Investment

Brooks C. Mendell, Ph.D.
Forisk Consulting

Forisk Press
Watkinsville, Georgia

Published by Forisk Press

For information about this book, contact:
  Forisk Consulting
  PO Box 5070
  Athens, GA 30604
  770.725.8447

Cover photos by Loren Mendell
Cover design by The Athens Printing Company
Illustrations by Max Lang

ISBN 978-0-9896150-2-0

Copyright © 2015 by Brooks C. Mendell

All rights reserved. No part of this book may be reproduced, stored in a retrieval system or transmitted in any form or by any means without permission in writing from the publisher.

Table of Contents

About this Book 5

Part I: Aunt Fanny Learns About Forestry as an Investment 8
    Aunt Fanny Tours Her Forest 8
    Aunt Fanny Asks About Forest Rotations 11
    Aunt Fanny Asks About the Value of Bare Land 13
        SIDEBAR: What is BLV and how is it useful for forest management? 16
    Aunt Fanny Asks About Timber Prices 17
    Aunt Fanny Asks About Cash Flow 20
    Aunt Fanny Asks About Timber Taxes 21
    Aunt Fanny Asks About Forestry Risks 23
        SIDEBAR: Why do we "prescribe" fire for forests? 27

Part II: Aunt Fanny Implements a Forest Management Plan 28
    Aunt Fanny Writes a Forest Management Plan 28
        Forest Management Plans: Outline to Discuss 30
    Excerpts from "Aunt Fanny's Forest Management Plan" 31
    Aunt Fanny Thins Her Forest 33
        SIDEBAR: Why do we "thin" forests? 36
    Aunt Fanny Learns About Cruising Timber 37
        SIDEBAR: Technical notes on timber cruising methods ... 40
    Aunt Fanny Learns More About Cruising and Forestry Consultants 40
        SIDEBAR: Resources for forest owners 45
    Aunt Fanny Discusses Communication and Managing Risk 46
    Aunt Fanny Prepares to Hire Forestry Professionals . 48
        SIDEBAR: Four steps to evaluate and hire forestry professionals. 49
        SIDEBAR: Questions to include in an interview guide 51

Part III: Aunt Fanny Considers Another Timberland Investment 53
    Aunt Fanny Discusses Timberland Returns 53

    Aunt Fanny Analyzes Her Timber Market 55
    Aunt Fanny Asks About Timber Prices, Again 57
    Aunt Fanny Asks About Forestland Appreciation 58
    Aunt Fanny Decides to Value a Forest 60

Conclusion 62
    Aunt Fanny's Ode to Forest Ownership 62

Checklists 65
    Investing in Timberland 65
    Basic Steps for Valuing a Forest 67

Glossary 69

References and Recommended Resources 74

Forestry and Forest Owner Associations by State 76

About the Author 84

About this Book

Acquiring, managing and selling timber and timberlands require specific skills to do so with minimum error and maximum profit. In this book, we learn with Aunt Fanny how to apply basic financial concepts in forestry when making decisions related to trading your cash and capital for tree-growing assets.

This book has been written with forest owners and timberland investors in mind; the lessons apply to owners and investors of all sizes. The book attempts to clarify the true risks and opportunities associated with forestland investments while prioritizing the questions to ask when developing and implementing an asset management plan. It does not bridge the skill or knowledge gap between amateurs and forestry professionals, but helps to organize your thinking when managing a forest. To the extent that this book also helps forestry consultants and management professionals educate and support their clients…super.

My grandmother, the late Frances Collat Mendell, inspired the character of Aunt Fanny. My Dad, the oldest of four children born and raised in Palo Alto, California, said she was one of the smartest folks in the family. Born on July 19, 1916 in New York, she attended UC Berkeley for two years before dropping out when her father fell ill.

Grandma Frances enjoyed salty jokes. While living in Macon, Georgia and working as a forester in the 1990s, I attended minor league baseball and hockey games. The local hockey team, the Macon Whoopee – the name still makes me smile – had, of course, the best selling t-shirt in the league. I mailed one to Grandma and she wore it. Often.[1] Laughing to the end, Grandma Frances passed away at age 92 in California. This book is dedicated to her.

---

[1] It runs in the family. My Dad wore the Hooters t-shirt I sent him from Macon until it literally disintegrated off his back.

Aunt Fanny is sharp, loves a good joke, wants to learn and enjoys making a little money. However, her recently inherited forestland remains a bit of a mystery to her. This book follows Aunt Fanny through her learning of the key concepts and ideas needed to manage her forest as an investment.

The book has three sections. In the first, Aunt Fanny gets to know her forest and learns about forestry and forest investments. In the second section, Aunty Fanny implements a forest management plan and prepares to hire professionals to help her. In the third section, Aunt Fanny considers another forest investment by investigating the neighboring forest, which is for sale.

The book includes supplementary resources. Checklists summarize key concepts. A glossary captures and defines selected terms. "References and Recommended Resources" lists articles, books and websites that offer additional, detailed information on topics covered in the book. Finally, a section on "Forestry and Forest Owner Associations" lists organizations and contact information by state so readers can reach out directly to local resources with forestry expertise.

We all want fair value for our labors, and a fair return on our capital. What better examples have we than investing in land and forests? The discipline and understanding required to earn long-term profits from forestland apply to any worthwhile venture. A practical forest owner looks at each investment decision as a series of small steps, with each closing the gap towards our final objectives.

The production of this book would not have been possible without the support and editorial suggestions of my friends and colleagues at Forisk: Amanda Lang, Heather Clark and Shawn Baker. Amanda's husband, Max Lang, lent his artistic talent to provide the artwork. And my brother Loren Mendell took the cover photographs while visiting me on a forestry job near Macon, Georgia in the 1990s. Thank you!

Finally, the freedom and inspiration to write, teach and grow a forestry research business would not be possible without the love and understanding of my wife, Liz, and daughters, Dani and Ellery. Thank you. You are the most important people in my life.

As my grandfather Will Mendell often said, "Life is what you make it." Enjoy the book, know your forest and love your family. Thank you for reading!

Part I: Aunt Fanny Learns About Forestry as an Investment

Aunt Fanny Tours Her Forest

At 4:14 in the morning, I woke up, rolled over and turned off the alarm before it chimed. At 4:15, the phone buzzed.

"Good morning, Nephew!" said Aunt Fanny. "You up?"

"Yes, Ma'am," I said, swinging my legs over the bed and slipping my feet into the cool fleece inside the moccasins on the floor. "I'm up and getting dressed. Meet at the gate in an hour?"

"I'll be there!"

# # #

At 5:10 am, I pulled up to where the woods road met the county road near Murder Creek. A fading yellow metal swing gate blocked the entrance to the forest. I stepped out of the truck to unlock the gate and swing it open.

A red Datsun 280ZX pulled up near the gate and parked on the side of the road. A middle-aged woman wearing aviator sunglasses and a single-piece camouflage jumpsuit stepped out of the car. She held a black-and-white marbled composition notebook and a calculator.

"Good morning, Aunt Fanny. Ready to go?"

"You bet, Nephew."

"Let's get into my truck."

# # #

Aunt Fanny, who retired after 30 plus years with a regional community bank, inherited 220 acres of forestland in middle Georgia. She called me a few weeks ago, primed with a list of questions.

"Nephew, it's my belief **you earn more if you learn more**, so I want to study this forest. Can you help me?" she asked over the phone.

"Yes, Ma'am," I said. She wanted to get a sense for how 'hands-on' she could or should be. She wanted to visit her forest with me to ask questions, look around and better understand how things work.

"High level, Nephew, what's required?" she asked on the phone that day. "I figure, unlike a shotgun wedding, forestry requires planning."

"Well, I hadn't thought of it that way before," I said before describing the basic process for putting a plan together for managing a forest as an investment.

"First, you define your objectives. Then, we assess your forest and land to understand what you've got. Then, given the forest you've got, we outline a few approaches to meet your objectives. Then, we decide on which approach. And finally we set up a schedule of forest management activities to implement the plan."

"Whew," she said on the other end of the line. "Then we go back to the house for a Wild Turkey refresher!"

"Yes, Ma'am," I said. "The nice thing about your forest is that it will grow and cycle with or without our help. But a management plan helps us keep the forest healthy and productive. A healthy forest can better handle insects and diseases and fire. And a managed forest can better meet your objectives."

"Well said, Nephew. When can we go visit my forest?"

#   #   #

After two hours of driving through the forest and getting a sense for its health and condition, I pulled into a small clearing near an old hunting stand and parked the truck. From behind the seat, I pulled out my Star Wars thermos and poured two cups of coffee, handing one to Aunt Fanny.

"Nephew, talk to me. How is this forest going to make me money?" she asked.

"If you need money today, we can cut and sell trees, or we can sell the land. Do you need money now?"

"No, no. And I want to keep the land. It's been in the family since my grandfather won it in a poker game. It's just that now I get to manage it. And, as you know, I hate idle assets."

Aunt Fanny had started out as a secretary at a local community bank. She worked her way up and retired as a regional vice president, managing bank branches throughout middle Georgia. Aunt Fanny knew her numbers.

"Okay, well let's go over a few basics. Think of your forest of trees as an army of soldiers," I said. "It's a factory full of workers looking to produce on your behalf."

"You're talking my language."

"The challenge is to put them to work on the right things, for the right length of time, with the proper nutrition while protecting them from bugs, fire and disease."

"Okay."

"Over time, your trees grow in size and quality and, most importantly, value. But at some point in the future, that growth in value slows down to a point where you'd be making more money by selling the trees and putting the money in something else. So the goal here is to grow the forest to its point of maximum value in today's dollars. Then we harvest that forest and start all over."

"Got it," said Aunt Fanny. "Maximize the present value of the forest, is that what you're telling me, Nephew?"

"Yes, Ma'am."

"How exactly does the value of a forest increase? Just by growing bigger trees?"

"Setting aside the land for now, **tree value changes from three things**. One, volume. The trees get bigger so we have more to sell. Two, quality. The trees get more valuable as they grow from smaller, less valuable products like pulpwood into larger, more valuable logs for sawmills and plywood facilities. Three, prices."

"How can you separate prices from quality? Sounds like you're selling me the same story twice, Nephew."

"Well, the thing is that prices can go up. And prices can go down. Depends on the market. So just because we're growing better trees, it doesn't guarantee more value for each 'unit' of tree. You see, together we know we can grow more trees and we can grow better trees, but we can't control the prices. So I wanted to be clear about what we can and can't control."

"A cautious young man. You'd have been a good banker," said Aunt Fanny, patting me on the shoulder.

"At the end of the day, the key question for us is 'when should we harvest this forest?' We have to figure out the 'optimal rotation' to maximize its value."

Aunt Fanny Asks About Forest Rotations

Aunt Fanny reached into the side pocket of her one-piece camouflage jumpsuit. She pulled out a blue roll of Mentos. "Want one?" she asked.

"Sure," I said, pinching off a white mint from the tin-foiled roll and popping it into my mouth. Aunt Fanny and I stared out into the woods, chewing our Mentos.

"Minty," I said.

"You ever put one of these in a bottle of Coke?" asked Aunt Fanny. "It's fantastic. Blows out a stream of foam like a water cannon. I saw it on YouTube."

I nodded, wondering where this was going.

"Nephew, you mentioned 'optimal rotation' a while ago," she said. "Only place I've heard that before was at the bowling alley. What are we talking about here?"

"It refers to our best estimate of when the forest is mature."

Aunt Fanny laughed. "When is a forest 'mature'?" she asked, making quotes in the air with her hands.

"Well, it depends on your goals. In forestry, we either try to maximize wood volume or we try to maximize value," I said.

"Don't they tell us the same thing?" asked Aunt Fanny.

"Surprisingly, no," I said. "We could grow a lot more volume if we didn't care about how much it would cost, how long it would take or what products we'd grow. But we do care about these things. So **we want to estimate the forest rotation that gets us the highest, sustainable economic returns**. The forest rotation age that makes the most money forever."

"Amen," said Aunt Fanny. "How do we figure this out? Magic 8 ball?"

"Ouija board," I said.

Aunt Fanny laughed. "Nice," she said. "Quick like your mother."

"Actually, we do some math," I said. "Since we want to prioritize economic returns, we will think about financial maturity."

"This is language I understand. Just like with bonds or CDs at the bank," said Aunt Fanny.

"Yes, in a way. We care about the rate of return. **A forest reaches financial maturity when its annual growth rate in value equals the target rate of return** or your cost of capital."

"Tell me more."

"Well, think about how a forest grows. When the trees are small and young, they have little value to mills. Then, as they start growing and adding size, they start to increase in value. Quickly. Then, eventually at some point, forest growth slows down, as does the annual increase in forest value."

"Makes sense," said Aunt Fanny. "Let's put some numbers to this. If I expect my forest to return 6% per year on average, I should let it grow as long as it continues to add value at a rate of 6% or more."

"Exactly," I said. "At some point, you have a mature forest full of sawlogs that's pretty valuable but increasing value at only 2% or 4%. You can keep growing it, but you would be 'losing' value because you could harvest, replant, and grow a new forest that returns 6% or more per year."

"And this takes time," said Aunt Fanny, looking into the woods.

"A lot of time," I said. "And that gets us back to estimating the optimal forest rotation. And to do this, **we need to know the value of bare land**. The value of dirt."

"Sounds like we have more to talk about," said Aunt Fanny.

"Yes, Ma'am."

Aunt Fanny Asks About the Value of Bare Land

Aunt Fanny sighed loudly and kicked the dirt. A pinecone ricocheted off a nearby white oak before landing in a mound of dirt and leaves. Two dogs barked in the distance.

"Nephew, I have a few thoughts regarding the value of land."

"Yes?" I asked.

"When I worked at the bank, we liked making loans for investments in buildings because these generated cash and provided reliable collateral," said Aunt Fanny, recalling her days as a regional vice president for a community bank.

"Yes, **real assets produce**," I said.

"Exactly," said Aunt Fanny. "So a building, for example, had some value no matter who owned it." And then she paused and raised her finger to make a point. "BUT the building had more value if managed well. It required less maintenance, earned higher rents and stayed occupied more consistently with reliable tenants."

I waited while Aunt Fanny caught her breath and toed the dirt again. The dogs had stopped barking, perhaps to listen.

"Nephew, how does this work with forestland?" she asked. "How do we value the land?"

"Well, what you said for the building holds, in a way, for forestland," I said. "A well-managed forest creates more income."

"Tell me more," said Aunt Fanny. "From an investment point of view."

"Okay," I said. "The value of the forestland relates to the income it generates from, mostly, growing trees. Basically, if one piece of land with a good management plan can grow more merchantable trees over time than another piece of land, the first has more value as an investment."

"You figure this out yourself?" asked Aunt Fanny.

"A German forester named Martin Faustmann figured it out in 1849."

"Who is this Martin fellow?" she asked. "I love history."

"He was a forester and an appraiser. One day he read an article about forest valuation that made him scratch his head," I said. "The author argued that forestland is worth the income you earn from a single rotation."

"Well that doesn't make sense," said Aunt Fanny. "It's like saying a building is worth the income from the first lease."

"Yes, if the first lease was for 20 or 30 years," I said. "Faustmann's insight was that after you harvest, you would replant and grow a second forest and then a third forest and so on. Each of those forests has value that should be reflected in the current price."

"But those trees probably won't generate cash for me," said Aunt Fanny. "They would happen in 50 years!"

"That's true, but they still have value, even if just a few percent of the total in today's dollars," I said. "It's an opportunity cost associated with owning the land."

"I guess that's right."

"Faustmann wrote up and published a different technique for valuing bare forestland, or 'dirt,' for tax purposes,"

14

I said. "And to this day, Faustmann's formula – referred to as 'bare land value' or 'BLV' or 'land expectation value' – remains a standard model for estimating the optimal timber rotation age and maximizing forest value in short and long-term analysis."

"Nephew, that was too much lecture and not enough entertainment," said Aunt Fanny.

"Well what did the monkey say when he caught his tail in the lawnmower?"

"What?" ask Aunt Fanny.

"Won't be long now," I said, matter of fact.

"Oh, Nephew," groaned Aunt Fanny. "No soup for you!"

"Sorry," I said. "Anyway, Faustmann's formula helped shape forest economics as we know it."

"My experience with formulas and models is that they are usually wrong," said Aunt Fanny, raising an eyebrow at me Spock-like.

"Yes, that's true, too," I said. "So we use 'bare land value' with caution. **BLV serves us best as a guide.** It takes our best information and assumptions, and lets us make comparisons between forest management plans or different properties."

"It's a tool in the toolbox. I get it," said Aunt Fanny.

"That's right," I said. "And some say that Faustmann, with this analysis, was one of the first to correctly use compound interest rates in discounted cash flow analysis. As a forester, I'm proud that another forester was a pioneer in analyzing real estate investments."

"I can see why," said Aunt Fanny. "He figured out the value of dirt."

SIDEBAR: What is BLV and how is it useful for forest management?

Bare land value (BLV) is a special application of net present value (NPV) that lets us compare forestry investments of different rotation lengths. BLV also helps identify the forest rotation (age) that maximizes the value of the forest. It uses assumed timber prices, forest management costs and interest rates to estimate the rotation that maximizes the value of the land when growing trees. BLV remains a standard financial measure for analyzing forest management alternatives.

BLV helps evaluate forestry investments with different rotations. For example, we can compare the strategies of managing for sawtimber versus managing for pulpwood. How does a forestland owner compare the costs and benefits of managing an 18-year rotation forest to a 31-year rotation forest? In finance, this 13-year gap between 18 and 31 creates a problem for apples-to-apples analysis which BLV neatly solves by assuming you manage the forest "in perpetuity" under different strategies.

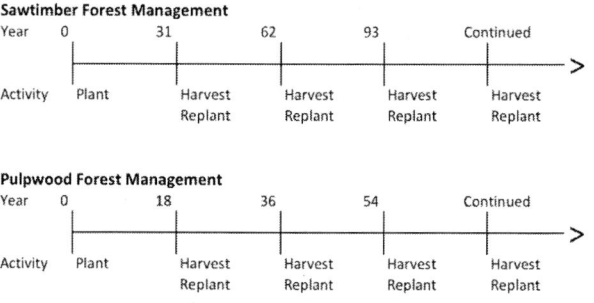

In short, BLV helps (1) identify the optimal rotation length for a forest; (2) schedule forest management activities; and (3) determine whether or not to invest in specific forest management (silvicultural) activities.

> Source: *"Forisk Finance Simplified"* published by Forisk Press.

Aunt Fanny Asks About Timber Prices

Aunt Fanny adjusted her aviator sunglasses, put her hands on her hips and looked up at the loblolly pine tree in front of her. "Nephew, talk to me about timber prices. What's this pine tree worth?"

I looked up towards the top of the tree. Then I stepped past Aunt Fanny to the base of the tree while pulling out the logger's tape hooked to my belt.

"What's that?" asked Aunt Fanny. She plucked a silver Cross pen from the front pocket of her camouflage jumpsuit and opened her marbled composition notebook to write something down.

"This is a logger's tape," I said. "We use it to measure log lengths or, like here, we use it as a D-tape, a diameter tape, to measure a tree's DBH. Diameter at breast height."

"Whoa, hold it there, Nephew. How does that work? My breasts are lower to the ground than yours! Seems like we'd be getting different measurements."

"Well, we typically measure DBH at four and a half feet off the ground, no matter how tall, or short, you are. The key is we want to be high enough off the ground to avoid measuring the butt swell of the tree."

"Whoa, again! Breast height? Butt swell? You're not talking to Joan Rivers here, Nephew."

I laughed. "Different trees have different shapes, just like people. So we try to measure their size in as consistent a way as possible. This, along with tree height, helps us estimate their volume, which tells us how much wood we've got to sell," I said. "Trees are typically thicker or wider at their base. This is the butt of the tree, which can mislead us on how much wood we've actually got here."

Aunt Fanny slowly scanned the tree from the base near the ground up into the branches of the crown. "I see how the tree gets skinnier up near the top. It's like a super stretched-out candy corn."

"Why don't you try this D-tape and measure the tree," I said reaching into my pocket to pull out a small metal D-tape.

"Sounds good, Nephew." I pulled out the tape 20 inches from its case and handed it to Aunt Fanny. She handed me her pen and notebook, and took the tape. "I'm five-foot two, so four and a half feet off the ground should be about at my mouth or nose. Sound right?"

"Yes, Ma'am."

Aunt Fanny reached around the tree and wrapped the tape around so both ends met in front of her, even with her mouth. "Says here 11 inches. What does that tell us?"

"This tree here is pretty straight and about 50 feet tall," I said. "No obvious defects such as forks low in the stem or big cankers or cavities. And it's big enough for a sawmill to cut some lumber. At 11 inches, in this local market, we'd call this a 'chip-n-saw' tree. It's a small sawlog."

"Chip-n-saw?" said Aunt Fanny. "The name sounds backwards to me."

"It refers to the mill technology. A 'chip-n-saw' mill specializes in cutting these smaller logs. While they will cut some lumber from the log, a decent portion of it will be chipped up and sent to a pulp mill for making paper. A 'chip-n-saw' machine can do the sawing and chipping at basically the same time."

"Sounds like tree purgatory," said Aunt Fanny. "Big enough to get in the door, but not quite big enough to be fully appreciated by the mill."

"Well, that's the thing with timber prices. They take into account how the tree gets used," I said.

"What do you mean?"

"Here in this market, trees get sold by the ton. A chip-n-saw tree is worth about $20 per ton. If the tree had a major defect and couldn't get sold to a sawmill, we'd send the entire stem to a pulp mill for about $10 per ton."

"What if we got out of purgatory and had a bigger tree?" asked Aunt Fanny.

"With a DBH above 12 inches, trees become 'sawtimber' and can go to sawmills that focus on lumber production. They could pay $30 per ton or more, depending on the size and quality."

"So bigger is better in forestry," she said. "That right, Nephew?"

"For the most part, yes, Aunt Fanny. As long as we get there in a reasonable amount of time."

I paused and looked around at the other trees. "Nephew, your wheels are turning. What's the rest of the story?"

"Well, if we focus too much on per ton prices, we forget the key value drivers under our control. **Per unit timber prices provide an incomplete view of timberland investments.**"

"Nephew, prices are important. I care about the price of milk for my Shredded Wheat, the price of gas for my 280ZX and the price of Wild Turkey for my afternoon snack. Surely timber prices matter."

"Yes, of course. I just wanted to put the prices in context. **Today's timber price is a function of today's technology and yesterday's timber price is a function of yesterday's technology.** Sawmills are more efficient, and forests are more productive."

"So you're saying my customer needs less wood and I'm producing more? That does not sound like favorable economics," said Aunt Fanny in her 'banker' voice.

"There's a lot going on here. Mills and foresters are constantly adapting to each other. Prices go up and down over time, but we get a sense for averages and baselines. For your forest, when thinking about the returns, **it's really about cash flow per acre per year**. And land appreciation, if any."

Aunt Fanny Asks About Cash Flow

After measuring the diameter of the pine tree, Aunt Fanny handed the D-tape back to me. I returned her Cross pen and black-and-white marbled composition notebook. She opened the notebook and wrote down a few things.

"Nephew, tell me more about how my forest generates cash. Isn't it just about getting higher prices for the trees we're growing?"

"There's a little more to it, Aunt Fanny."

"Always is," she said, smiling.

"Let's talk about what our cash flows look like and where they come from."

"This is not a beauty pageant, Nephew. All incoming cash flows look good to me. They don't need to be from Brazil in a bikini."

"Right," I said, pausing a moment to let that image pass. "Well, first, **income from harvesting your forest is periodic**. We don't cut trees every quarter or every year for smaller properties. If you owned thousands of acres, we might have enough different age classes where we'd cut and sell some trees somewhere on the property each year. But not in this case."

"So when do we cut trees for sale?"

"Typically, we'll do a thinning when the trees are between 15 and 18 years old, and we'll do a final harvest, a clear cut, between age 25 and 30, depending on the trees, on the market and on your financial needs."

"Then we replant and grow a new forest?"

"Right. We do have to spend money to replant, so we take some of that income and reinvest it into the forest."

"Makes sense," said Aunt Fanny while writing in her notebook.

"Second, those **cash flows from harvesting are diversified**. We'll be selling different products, such as pulpwood logs to pulp mills and sawlogs to sawmills, and we'll be selling different species, like pine and hardwoods."

"Never liked all my eggs in one basket. Sounds good, Nephew."

"Third, **the forest also generates smaller, more regular cash flows** from things like hunting leases or harvesting pine straw." I paused to let Aunt Fanny think.

"It sounds like the cash flow from the final harvest is pretty important. Break it down for me, Nephew."

"Yes, Ma'am, that's right. Cash flows come mostly from the price of the forest products you're growing multiplied by the volume of each product harvested."

"Makes sense. Like farming. Price X times my bushels of corn and price Y times my bales of hay."

"Right. Except in forestry, our volume, the amount and type of forest products we grow changes over time. Forest management improves and mills change what they want. Technology in action."

"Well, that's not much different than farming, Nephew, is it? Technology changes all of the time."

"That's true, except with farming you can adjust each year by changing the crops," I said. "In forestry, we're making decisions today for trees we'll harvest in 15 or 25 years."

Aunt Fanny looked into the woods. "So you're saying I'm growing cash flows for another day."

"It depends. Here, we have some mature timber that we could harvest today. But if you're starting fresh, yes, we're 'planting a business' that produces its biggest cash flows in the future," I said. "A friend of mine, another forester, always says 'in forestry, we're in the delayed gratification business'."

Aunt Fanny Asks About Timber Taxes

We got back into my truck and rode down the woods road. I glanced over at Aunty Fanny in the passenger seat. She opened her black-and-white marbled composition notebook on her lap and ran her finger down the page. Then she looked out the driver side window into the woods and said, "Tell me about taxes."

"You'll have to pay some," I said.

"Nephew," said Aunt Fanny shaking her head, "any Padawan knows that."

I laughed and nodded my head. "Forests do provide different kinds of tax incentives to landowners, depending on how you're set up and where you're located," I said.

"You have my attention," said Aunt Fanny.

"Well, you've got reforestation tax credits. You can also qualify for long-term capital gains treatment. And you can participate in different state and federal programs designed for forestry and conservation."

"Like what?"

"For example, some states, like Georgia, allow forest owners to enroll their forests in conservation programs that reduce annual property taxes," I said. "If you plan to hold and manage your land for forestry, it can be a good deal."

Aunt Fanny sat quietly as we rumbled down the graveled road. "Nephew, you've worked with a lot of forest owners. What kinds of mistakes do people make when it comes to taxes?"

"Number one is that they overpay. They pay more in taxes than they probably need to," I said.

"Taxes are complicated, Nephew," said Aunt Fanny.

"They are complicated, but not THAT complicated," I said. "If my clients do nothing else, I tell them to know their basis, which is what you've got invested in the timber. Keep a file with all of the receipts and contracts and documentation. And then, before tax season, hire, or at least talk to, an accountant who understands timber well enough to provide some guidance."

"Are taxes different for timber?" asked Aunt Fanny.

"Different enough," I said. "A few years ago, one of my clients missed out on thousands of dollars of deductible expenses because his accountant was unfamiliar with tax code changes for reforestation expenses."

"Ouch," said Aunt Fanny.

"Just confirm that your accountant has timber experience and keep up with your files."

"In other words, stay organized and confirm credentials," said Aunt Fanny, nodding her head.

"Exactly," I said. "And your accountant will thank you. You don't want to lose the proof you need for the IRS that shows you are managing your forest as a business or investment."

"Why does that matter?" asked Aunt Fanny.

"Well, the IRS cares about the 'nature of your ownership,'" I said, making quotes in the air with my fingers. "If you own a forest, first and foremost, for recreation, then the IRS would view your forest as a 'personal use property' rather than as an investment for profit."

"Nephew, profit and pleasure do not seem like conflicting goals!" said Aunty Fanny.

"No, you're right," I said. "However, the distinction has tax consequences. So staying organized will help ensure you only pay what's required, and not a penny more."

"There's a lot to know here as a forest owner, it sounds like," said Aunt Fanny.

"There are good resources," I said. "I always recommend the website 'www.timbertax.org' which has about everything you need in one place, including good materials published by the USDA Forest Service."

"I'll check it out," said Aunt Fanny, writing in her composition notebook.

"At the end of the day, we want to pay as little as possible under the law," I said. "A wise woman once told me, 'avoiding guilt is easy. Don't cheat on your spouse, your expense report or your taxes.'"

"Good memory, Nephew," said Aunt Fanny.

Aunt Fanny Asks About Forestry Risks

Aunt Fanny leaned back against the side of my truck while I refilled our cups with coffee from my Star Wars thermos. We both blew on the coffee in our cups to cool it down.

Staring through the steam rising from her cup, Aunt Fanny said, "Nephew, that is one serious fire ant condominium complex right over there." She pointed to a two-foot wide dirt mound at the edge of the woods road a few yards from where I parked.

"Yes, Ma'am. That may be the fire ant Trump Plaza," I said, sipping my coffee.

"What's the risk to my forest from those ants?" asked Aunt Fanny.

"In established forests like this one, not much," I said. "Fire ant colonies like these tend to show up near roads like this. Near man-made disturbances."

Aunt Fanny nodded.

"But don't step in one," I added.

"Oh, that was helpful, Nephew. What would I do without you?"

I laughed, taking another sip of coffee.

"So what risks should I worry about?" asked Aunt Fanny. "Help me put everything into perspective."

"Alright," I said. "Let's start with fur, fire and felons."

"Sounds interesting."

"Well, if all you knew abut forestry came from the front pages of the newspaper, you'd think our forests were full of furry endangered species, fires blazing out of control and felons hiding dead bodies, growing marijuana and running meth labs."

"This sounds exciting," said Aunt Fanny. "Time to call Special Agent Gibbs at NCIS!"

"It would be exciting for television, but it's less interesting if it's happening on your forest."

"Good point, Nephew," said Aunt Fanny. "I got carried away thinking about Mark Harmon. Love that man."

"Well, the good news is that these risks, while real, can be overblown a bit in the papers," I said. "Overall, things like fires and insects and endangered species affect a small percent of the acres each year in privately-owned working forests."

"Nephew, you're starting to sound like a professor again," said Aunt Fanny. "How should I think about risks to my forest here in front of us?"

"Well, there are basically four buckets of timberland risks," I said, as Aunt Fanny put down her coffee cup and pulled out her Cross pen.

"Okay, ready, Professor" she said, opening her black-and-white marbled composition notebook.

"First, you've got your physical risks like fire, insects and disease," I said. "These affect the volume and quality of your trees."

"Got it."

"Second, you've got financial risks from things like changing timber prices, which affect your revenues, and changing costs for things we pay for like fertilizer and seedlings."

"Okay, got it."

"Third, we have operational risks. Basically things like weather and access to the trees. Issues that affect our daily forest management activities."

"Okay, I'm still with you," said Aunt Fanny, writing in her notebook.

"Finally, there are regulatory risks from things like changing land use laws and tax policies. Even certification."

Aunt Fanny made a few more notes. "Okay, Nephew, let me recap. My four buckets of risk are physical, financial, operational and regulatory."

"You got it."

"That was definitely like being back in a classroom," said Aunt Fanny. "Time for questions?"

"Please raise your hand," I said in a deep voice.

"Cute. Don't we use fire sometimes to manage the forest?"

"Yes, absolutely," I said. "Prescribed fire is a standard forest management practice, especially in pine stands."

"That's what I thought," said Aunt Fanny. "Still got my grandfather's drip torch."

"Hold on to that one," I said to Aunt Fanny. "It's a classic."

"And what about someone stealing my timber? How do you think about timber theft?"

"Well, I think of it as a physical risk because of the way we manage against it," I said. "Basically, these risks that affect our trees directly require vigilance. We need a process to prevent and minimize and respond. These risks never go away, but we can squeeze them down. That's true for theft like it is for fire and diseases."

Aunt Fanny nodded her head and closed her notebook. "That's a lot to think about, Nephew."

"I like to remind myself that risk has two faces," I said.

"What the heck does that mean?" asked Aunt Fanny.

"Well, it means **'risk' does not mean good or bad,**" I said. "**It just refers to changes that we may or may not be able to control.** So we put things in perspective, make a plan and do the best we can."

SIDEBAR: Why do we "prescribe" fire for forests?

We burn forests "by design" to improve forest health and reduce the potential for extreme wildfires. Forest ecosystems that require periodic fires but fail to get them will build up flammable fuels while suppressing fire-dependent tree species.

When managing forests as an investment, prescribed burning improves returns by reducing competition for water, nutrients and sunlight from less "desirable" trees and plants. This improves the size and quality of the trees you plan to harvest and market. Burning can also benefit wildlife by improving access to and through forests for quail and deer, and by keeping vegetation at "usable" heights for foraging.

The USDA Forest Service (www.fs.fed.us/fire/management/rx.html) notes that prescribed fire can:
- *Reduce hazardous fuels, protecting human communities from extreme fires;*
- *Minimize the spread of pest insects and disease;*
- *Remove unwanted species that threaten species native to an ecosystem;*
- *Provide forage for game;*
- *Improve habitat for threatened and endangered species;*
- *Recycle nutrients back to the soil; and*
- *Promote the growth of trees, wildflowers, and other plants.*

Burning can be dangerous. Work with certified burners or specialists who will prepare and implement burn plans that account for temperature, wind, smoke and other factors.

Part II: Aunt Fanny Implements a Forest Management Plan

Aunt Fanny Writes a Forest Management Plan

Aunt Fanny and I walked away from the truck and down the woods road for another 50 or 60 yards. We stopped at an earthen hump that angled across the road.

"Looks like someone built a crooked speed bump," said Aunt Fanny, looking down at the mound with her hands on the hips of her camouflage jumpsuit.

"It's an old water bar," I said. "It helps manage the flow of water from rain storms. See how there's another one down the road a ways?" I pointed toward another, similar looking hump in the road.

"Yes, I see it. How do they work?" asked Aunt Fanny.

"Well, they protect this unpaved road by deflecting and reducing the flow of water, which also prevents erosion and sedimentation," I said. "Keeps the dirt on the road and out of the brush."

"So it IS a speed bump," said Aunt Fanny. "It reduces water accidents."

"I guess that's right," I said, laughing. "You win."

We continued walking down the road. Aunt Fanny stopped, and looked up and down the rocky dirt road. Then she opened up her black-and-white marbled composition notebook and flipped to the first few pages. "Several weeks ago, when we spoke on the phone, you told me about forest management planning."

'Yes, Ma'am, that's right," I said.

"You outlined a few steps," said Aunt Fanny, as she moved her finger down a list on a page in her notebook. "Define your objectives. Assess your forest. Outline a few approaches to meet your objectives. Pick an approach. Then set it up and implement. Sound about right?"

"Sounds like you're a good note taker and sounds like I'd be smart to watch what I say around you."

"Well, that goes without saying, Nephew."

"Yes, Aunt Fanny, you captured it," I said. "As you noted, **the key question to answer up front is 'what do I want from my forest?'** Big buckets include things like investment returns or cash, wood production, recreation, and conservation. There are others, too."

"I only get to choose one?" asked Aunt Fanny.

"No, not at all. These are not 'mutually exclusive', as they say," I said making quotes in the air with my hands. "But we do need to prioritize. As Confucius said, 'If you chase two rabbits, you catch none.'"

"Confucius never saw me in action with my Benelli," said Aunt Fanny.

"That may be," I said. "But even Annie Oakley had to pick one to shoot first."

"Okay, you may be right about that," said Aunt Fanny, smiling.

"Besides, this choice is not a set of handcuffs. We can modify objectives over time," I said. "We just need a clear place to start for mapping out a plan."

"Makes sense."

"Identifying your objectives gives everyone, including your forester, guidance and direction," I said.

"Is it enough to say that my objective is to maximize the value of my forest?" asked Aunt Fanny. "For me, this is, first and foremost, an investment."

"That gets us started," I said. "I might ask a few questions about whether you want to maximize long-term profits or near-term cash flows. Or you may have a goal of maximizing tax credits or returns in your overall portfolio, of which this forest may simply be a part."

"This can get complicated, I see," said Aunt Fanny.

"Yes, Ma'am, it can," I said. "If we let it. I try to get crystal clear about the objective, and then outline a plan that has some flexibility. Things change. They always do."

"Sounds practical, Nephew," said Aunt Fanny.

"And I like taking a practical approach to coming up with ideas for the plan," I said. "For example, we may want to talk with your neighbors over there and see what plans they have. To start with, it's good to know your neighbors. And second, it helps to know if they have objectives that line up with what you want or if we may have to work around something."

"Nephew, you're motivating me to get started," said Aunt Fanny. "Tell me more about what's in a forest management plan."

"I was waiting for that," I said, reaching into the breast pocket of my Ben Davis work shirt. I pulled out a folded piece of paper. "We've gotta know what you have before we plan and make decisions. Here's an outline of the key parts."

Forest Management Plans: Outline to Discuss

State Objectives
- Clearly!

Describe Resources
- Quantify inventories
- Describe stands
- Maps

Describe Local Timber Market
- List local mills

Recommend Forest Management Activities
- Schedule by year (timeline)
- Note how these meet objectives

Discuss Cash Flows (Financial Analysis)
- Harvest schedule (wood flows by year)
- Costs and revenues by year

Keep Records
- Useful info for taxes and planning

"Looks good to me," said Aunt Fanny. "Other resources I could check out besides your crumpled outline?"

I laughed. "Yes, Ma'am. The U.S. Forest Service puts out a guide on the Internet that can help you think through a forest management plan. It's called 'Forest*A*Syst."

"Can you spell that?" asked Aunt Fanny, pulling out her Cross pen and marbled black-and-white composition notebook.

"Yes. The website is 'www.forestasyst.org'," I said, before spelling it out. "The website has lots of resources."

Aunt Fanny closed her notebook and nodded her head. "What's next, Nephew?"

"Let's go back to the truck, get some coffee and start making notes," I said. "Then you can check out those other resources when you get home, and we can talk again about writing up a plan for your forest."

"Sounds like a plan, Nephew."

Excerpts from "Aunt Fanny's Forest Management Plan"

The purpose of this management plan is to identify and evaluate the resources of Aunt Fanny's Forest in order to make recommendations based on her objectives and goals. These objectives include (in this order):
1) Improve forest health and timber growth;
2) Increase the long-term, sustainable financial returns from managing and growing trees; and
3) Enhance wildlife habitat.

Aunt Fanny's Forest includes 220 contiguous acres in Middle County, Georgia. The forest is divided into three distinct stands of timber. Aunt Fanny's Forest is located 7 miles north of Garrett, Georgia in Middle County on the east side of County Road 6B. The property has been in the family for three (3) generations. Aunt Fanny inherited the property this year.

Aunt Fanny's Forest

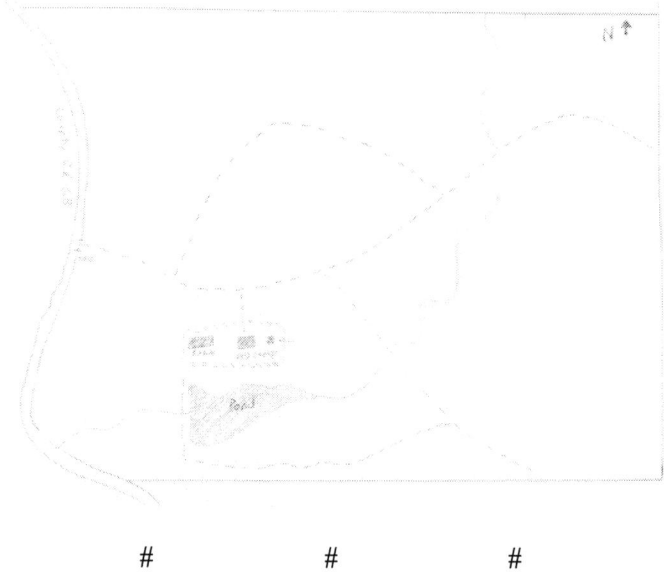

\# \# \#

Local timber markets within 100 road miles include seven (7) pine sawmills, two (2) pine plywood plants, one (1) pole plant, four (4) hardwood grade mills, two (2) pulp mills and four (4) chip mills. A list and map of these mills, along with a summary of their product specifications, are in the Plan's Appendix.

\# \# \#

The 220-acre tract consists of planted loblolly pine mixed with natural pine and natural hardwoods located along creeks. The property includes three different sections (stands) of timber. Recommended activities in this management plan include timber harvests (including thinnings), prescribed burning, reforestation, and food plot maintenance. The primary goal of these recommendations is to grow the largest and most valuable trees possible as soon as possible.

\# \# \#

TIMBER STAND 2: "Flatwood"
LOBLOLLY PINE (72 ACRES)

Planted in 1994, this loblolly pine stand has approximately 600 trees per acre with an average DBH (diameter) of 7 inches. The stand has even topography ideal for pine plantation management. This stand will be referred to as the Flatwood.

Recommendations
Flatwood (Stand 2) should be thinned this year to remove diseased, poorly formed and suppressed trees, including hardwood trees. The results of this harvest activity will be to (1) give the highest potential trees more space and resources, enabling them to grow bigger and faster; (2) increase forage for wildlife (deer, turkeys); and (3) generate a modest, interim cash flow.

The timeline and financial analysis associated with these recommendations are in the Plan's Appendix.

Aunt Fanny Thins Her Forest

Aunt Fanny and I stood on the woods road and looked through her forest of densely packed pine trees. Aunt Fanny removed her aviator sunglasses, folded them and put them in the front pocket of her camouflage jumpsuit.

She turned and looked into my eyes. "Nephew, how old am I?"

"You're 29," I said, without hesitating.

"Good boy. You're mother trained you well," said Aunt Fanny, putting her glasses back on and looking out into the woods. "Now tell me, how old are these trees?"

"Well, it's hard to say. Most of the trees we can see standing here are about the same size and age…"

Aunt Fanny cut me off. "Nephew, keep it short."

"These trees are 20 years old," I said.

"Thank you," she said. Like her Wild Turkey bourbon, Aunt Fanny likes her facts straight. "How do you know?" she asked, staring back out into the forest.

"It's my best guess based on the size, height and number of trees," I said.

"Nephew, what are we looking at? I see the trees, and I see the forest, but I don't see the issues."

"You've got yourself an overstocked stand of loblolly pine trees," I said.

"What does that mean?" she asked.

"You have too many trees," I said. "Your forest needs a thinning."

"How can I have too many trees?" she asked. "Seems to me more trees means more money."

"Well, it's like having too many flowers or weeds in the garden. There's only so much sunlight, water and nutrients to go around per acre," I said. "You have a lot of smallish, crowded trees. If your goal is to maximize value…" I paused.

"Yes, Nephew? You have my attention," said Aunt Fanny.

"If your goal is to maximize value and cash flow over the long-term, you're better off with fewer, larger and more valuable trees," I said. **"If your forest is an investment, thinning improves cash flows and returns**."

"Talk me through that," said Aunt Fanny, opening up her black-and-white marbled composition notebook to write.

"A thinning removes the smallest, weakest trees and leaves the straightest most promising trees. If done properly, it gives your best trees more room and nutrients. And then these trees grow through the product classes, from pulpwood to chip-n-saw to sawtimber, in less time."

"Sounds good."

"As one of my forestry professors said in school, 'you take the rest and leave the best.'"

"Cute, Nephew," said Aunt Fanny with a smirk. Then she wrote it down in her notebook. "Does thinning make me more money?"

"Yes."

"So why wouldn't everyone thin their forest?" asked Aunt Fanny.

"Well, a lot of folks do. And different folks have different objectives. You can thin for forest health reasons and you can thin for financial reasons. Or both. But some folks don't have enough forest to fool with."

"Will a thinning put cash in my pocket today?" asked Aunt Fanny. "I'm thinking of buying a new four-wheeler."

"Yes. A thinning generates some cash now from selling pulpwood and chip-n-saw trees. But the big payoff comes later, when we harvest the stand in six to ten years. Your forest will be full of higher value sawtimber."

"Delayed gratification again?" asked Aunt Fanny.

"Right. And **through harvesting trees periodically over time, we generate cash flows and financial returns from the forest**."

Aunt Fanny looked into the woods again. "Nephew, I keep thinking about those gaps in time between cash flows. What happens after we cut all the trees?"

"At that point, we'll need to spend money to replant," I said.

"How long between spending money on planting trees and generating cash again?" asked Aunt Fanny.

"At least fifteen years, or so," I said.

"You gotta have faith in this business."

"Yes, Ma'am, you speak the truth. The thing is, **your forest is one of thousands in this local market, each with its own range of ages and products**."

"But I don't care about everyone else, Nephew. I care about my investment here," said Aunt Fanny in her 'banker' voice.

"I understand, but think of it from the other side of the table," I said, picking up a stick from the ground and making a circle in the dirt at our feet.

"You always liked playing in the dirt, Nephew."

I pointed the stick to the middle of the circle. "Imagine a mill here that buys your trees. That mill does not care about you 99% of the time. They care about you during those two or three weeks once every 15 years or so when you have trees to sell. So you need all of those other landowners out there, planting and growing trees, to keep those mills interested and viable for all that time in between. It's really a relationship."

Aunt Fanny scanned the forest and then looked up towards the sky. "Good Lord, who taught my Nephew to talk like this?"

"It's how it works," I said, smiling. "**Time and location drive value in forestry.** You can't have a sawmill without forests, and it's hard to justify planting trees without mills nearby if you own your forest as an investment."

SIDEBAR: Why do we "thin" forests?

Active forest management often includes partial harvests called thinnings to remove poorly formed and diseased trees. For softwood plantations in particular, thinnings are a critical tool for maximizing the health and financial returns of a stand.

Foresters often employ "first" and "second" thinnings. First thinnings focus on removing weaker and smaller trees so that nutrients and other resources can flow to those remaining trees with the best growth potential. Thinning provides additional space for those trees to grow. Second thinnings look to identify and benefit the best "crop trees" to maximize the value of the forest. We remove the balance of the trees while also generating an interim source of cash by selling those trees to local mills.

In other words, we thin forests in order to grow the largest sized trees in as little time as possible. Why? Bigger trees have more value. The sooner we meet this objective, the higher the annualized returns for the landowner.

Thinnings also support wildlife management objectives. Thinning opens up a stand and allows sunlight to reach the ground. This encourages added vegetation growth in the understory that can attract wildlife.

Aunt Fanny Learns About Cruising Timber

As Aunt Fanny looked around and into the trees, her lips moved.

"Uh oh, she's lost it," I thought to myself. "What are you doing?" I asked.

"Counting trees," she said, as if it was the most natural and obvious thing to be doing when standing on the edge of a forest. Then Aunt Fanny pulled out her black and white marbled composition notebook, opened it up to a blank page and started making hash marks with her Cross pen to keep a tally.

"How many do you have so far?" I asked, after watching for a few minutes.

Aunt Fanny wrinkled her nose. "Not sure. Every time I look down to write in my notebook, I lose track of where I am in the woods when I look up again."

Out in the forest, a bird chirped. A dog barked. "Would you accept some help from your humble Nephew? He is an actual living and breathing forester."

Aunt Fanny chuckled. "Certainly. Explain to me how it's done, humble Nephew!"

"You are trying to conduct a critical and fundamental forest management activity. You are cruising your timber," I said.

"Nephew, I used to cruise Main Street in high school. And I went on a cruise once in Alaska. Who cruises timber? What does that mean?" asked Aunt Fanny.

"When foresters want to estimate the volume and, ultimately, the value of standing trees, they conduct what's called a 'timber cruise'," I said, making quotes in the air with my hands.

"This just sounds like another way of saying 'measure the forest'," said Aunt Fanny while also making quotes in the air with her hands.

"Yes, exactly," I said, smiling.

"This is hard," said Aunt Fanny, shaking her head and looking at the page in her notebook. "Why bother? I mean, just look around. There are more trees here than you can shake a stick at."

"Actually, a timber cruise gives us useful, even critical, information to help us manage a forest," I said. "It gives us an organized way to figure out where we are. It's a systematic estimate of the forest inventory."

"To make a plan, you gotta know where you are and where you want to go," said Aunt Fanny, nodding her head.

"Exactly. A timber cruise provides a baseline, a starting place, for figuring out what's here. Like you said, counting trees, especially when you try to do it for hundreds or thousands of acres, is hard."

"Tell me more about how this works," said Aunt Fanny, turning to a clean page in her notebook.

"Sure," I said. "We cruise the timber to help us value or manage a forest, so our goal is get a good handle on the number, size and distribution of trees."

"Okay, that makes sense," said Aunt Fanny.

"We also want to identify any other features in the forest that may affect our ability to manage the forest or harvest timber."

"Like what?" asked Aunt Fanny.

"Like are there places where trees are dying from bugs or disease? Are there gullies or streams or ponds? Are there old home sites with wells, historic artifacts or cemeteries?"

"Cemeteries? As in final resting place?"

"Yes, Ma'am," I said. "Depending on where we are in the country, we could find anything from old Indian mounds to gravesites from the Civil War."

"My grandfather used to find arrow heads all the time while walking the woods," said Aunt Fanny.

"Me, too," I said, pulling a chipped, pointed piece of flint from my pocket.

"Tell me more about how a timber cruise works," said Aunt Fanny. "And keep it simple, Professor."

"When we cruise, we take 'representative samples' from different locations throughout the forest. These locations are called plots. At each plot, your humble forester notes the key tree species, and estimates the number and size and quality of these trees."

"Okay, I'm with you," said Aunt Fanny, writing in her notebook. "So far."

"Great," I said. "Just remember that we can't know the value of your timber until we have a handle on the volume of timber by type on your property. So the cruise gives us a way to estimate the volume of pine logs and pulpwood and hardwood logs on your property."

Aunt Fanny nodded her head.

"To estimate the value of your timber, we multiply the volume for each product and specie by a price for that product."

"What about trees that we can't sell?" asked Aunt Fanny.

"Good point," I said. "Some volumes may be considered 'unmerchantable.' In other words, they have no commercial value. This might include small, damaged trees or species with no local market or volumes on areas that cannot be harvested. The timber cruise should account for this."

"What about baby trees?"

I laughed. "That's one name for them. We would call small, young trees 'pre-merchantable.' These trees are simply too young to harvest and sell, but they are important because they represent your future forest."

"And my future cash flows," said Aunt Fanny, finally looking up.

"Exactly."

SIDEBAR: Technical notes on timber cruising methods

We cruise a forest to determine the potential value of the timber on a site before conducting any management activity or business transaction (i.e. buying or selling timber or acres) that leads to a change of ownership. Timber cruises help foresters track forest growth and health. Regularly scheduled, systematic cruises or updates of the same forest help identify changing conditions in the forest related to insects, weather damage and timber theft.

Foresters draw on different methods when cruising timber. These include strip cruises, fixed-plot cruises, variable radius cruises (also known as a prism cruise), and 100% tally cruises. Strip, fixed-plot and variable radius approaches typically measure a sample of the trees in a forest. When implementing one of these approaches, the forester organizes the plots in a systematic and evenly distributed grid over the property to assess, as best as possible, the entire forest.

Aunt Fanny Learns More About Cruising and Forestry Consultants

      Aunt Fanny paused. She closed her black and white marbled composition notebook, put the Cross pen in the breast pocket of her camouflage jumpsuit, and slipped her aviator sunglasses from off the top of her head down to the bridge of her nose.

"Nephew," she said, "certain parts of managing a forest, like this timber cruising, feel a bit technical to me. I don't have the experience, yet, to know what I'm looking at or what to worry about. It will come down to the competence of my forester. And how much I trust him or her."

These were words and concerns I had heard before from other forest owners. Technical. Experience. Worry. Trust. And each person combined these words into their own story of wanting to get a handle on managing and enjoying their forest.

"Earth to Nephew," said Aunt Fanny, grabbing my elbow. "You still here?"

"Yes, yes, sorry," I said. "I've been thinking about what you said."

"Well, that's good," said Aunt Fanny. "So share."

"**Owning and managing a forest is a practical, doable thing**," I said. "And, at times, we make it sound more complicated than it is."

"What do you mean?" asked Aunt Fanny.

"For starters, if you did nothing and went on vacation to a deserted island for twenty years, your trees would still keep growing," I said. "You may not have the best quality trees and you may not have the highest volume of wood. A chance exists that bugs or disease, unchecked, could damage part of your forest. But overall, you'd still have a piece of land with a lot trees on it."

"Hmmmm. That actually makes me feel better," said Aunt Fanny.

"Now, if you want to improve financial returns and keep your forest healthy and productive, it helps to have a plan, and to implement it. And you have one."

"This is quite motivational, Nephew!"

"At the end of the day, the best things a timberland owner can do is get smart about the basics of forestry, including timber cruises, and get familiar with their local markets for timber and meet knowledgeable folks in their area," I said.

"So can we talk timber cruising again?" asked Aunt Fanny. "I have another question."

"Sure, of course," I said.

"What should I know, given that I'll never cruise timber myself?"

"Okay, there are specific things you can watch for and look for when reviewing a timber cruise," I said.

"Hold on a second," said Aunt Fanny, while pulling out her Cross pen and reopening her composition notebook. "Ready, Professor."

"First, double check the acres. In the old days, before we had satellites and GIS systems for digital maps, we could be wrong simply because we had the wrong number of acres," I said. "This is less of a problem now, but it helps to confirm that the forester cruised your 220 acres and not 120 acres or 320 acres."

"That makes sense," said Aunt Fanny. "Like checking the income line on your tax returns. 'Whoa, I didn't earn 3 million dollars last year! Whose tax returns are these?'"

"Second, make sure the cruise notes which acres are actually 'operable'," I said, making quotes with my hands. "You want to avoid counting and valuing volume that you could never harvest anyway. An extreme example would be trees on an island in the middle of a pond. From an investment standpoint, those trees don't have much value because you can't get to them."

"But I would still enjoy them," said Aunt Fanny.

"For sure," I said. "And so would the wildlife and birds. And, aesthetically, they add to your property. But they don't help your timber growing business."

"Okay, I get it," said Aunt Fanny while writing in her notebook.

"Third, double check assumptions in the cruise related to forest product specifications and prices in the local timber market. When your forester says 'you have 1,000 tons of sawtimber on your property', you just want to make sure the local sawmills would also call these same trees sawtimber. And compare the prices used in the cruise with other resources, like newsletters or extension foresters."

"Now I'm feeling overwhelmed, Nephew," said Aunt Fanny, making a show of writing in her notebook. As a former regional banker, it was hard to rattle Aunt Fanny. She knew her numbers and understood businesses and people.

"You're pulling my chain, Aunt Fanny."

Aunt Fanny smiled. "Well, maybe I am, but this is a lot of information. It's easy to say 'double check the prices,' but it's harder to do this when you've never done it before."

Aunt Fanny's words had me thinking again.

"Did my words have you thinking again?" asked Aunt Fanny.

"How did you know?" I said, smiling. "In the end, it comes down to becoming familiar with forestry and the services provided by the forestry professionals you hire."

"Do I have to hire a forestry consultant?" asked Aunt Fanny.

"No, you don't have to," I said. "But understand why you might or might not do this. Lots of good folks serve the forest industry, but sometimes a less scrupulous timber buyer or know-it-all neighbor might tell a new forest owner, 'you don't need to hire a forester. I've been in the woods and timber business all my life and can show you how to manage your land.' Then that leads to promises about prices and logging quality and all sorts of things."

"You're getting worked up, Nephew," said Aunt Fanny.

"Well, I've seen landowners get cheated," I said. "And on the other hand, an experienced, hard-working forester with good references can not only earn your trust, but also earn back any investment you make in his or her services and more."

"Makes sense," said Aunt Fanny.

"At the end of the day, it's still your forest. You can work with whomever you want and should not feel pressured to do anything," I said.

"Amen, Nephew," said Aunt Fanny. "Of course every deal has two sides. What should a forest owner know about forestry consultants?"

I laughed. "That's a first, Aunt Fanny! Thank you for asking."

"You're welcome," said Aunt Fanny. "Now answer, please."

"Yes, Ma'am. The thing with being a forester is it's a little like being a doctor or a lawyer. Once someone finds out what you do, they start asking questions about their situation," I said. "Does that make sense?"

"Oh, sure. When I worked at the bank, I never missed a chance for a third, fourth or fifth opinion on the pain in my side when one of our local doctors walked in," said Aunt Fanny. She paused. "Turns out my girdle was too tight."

"I'm pretending I didn't hear that," I said. "But, yes, it can be that way for foresters. People ask about the trees in their yard and the trees in their neighbor's yard that lean over their property."

Aunt Fanny started nodding her head. "Oh, sure. I've done both of those."

"And when a forest owner calls a forestry consultant for the first time to come out and visit their land, it's sort of understood that the first meeting is like a free consultation," I said. "You're getting to know each other."

"Right," said Aunt Fanny.

"Some folks take it too far, though," I said. "In most cases, a forest owner should compensate a forester who takes the time to visit and educate them. A two or three-hour discussion and walk through with a local forester will cover the health of your stand, local market conditions, recent issues related to bugs or disease and news related to other landowners or loggers. Frankly, this information is invaluable."

"I hear you, Nephew. So, what do I owe you for your time?" asked Aunt Fanny, looking up at me through her aviator sunglasses.

SIDEBAR: Resources for forest owners

Extension foresters: like county agents in agriculture, these professionals can walk you through your woods, highlight key issues and share educational publications. Also, extension foresters are usually affiliated with research universities that have forestry programs, so they would have access to current research and workshops.

Forest landowner groups: state and national associations provide readily accessible resources and support in the form of educational meetings, publications and lobbying or information on topics relevant to forest owners. Regional meetings also provide a useful way to meet and learn from other forest owners and forestry consultants. See "Forestry and Forest Owner Associations by State" at the back of this book for a list.

Timber market reports and research reports: states with forestry agencies or departments of natural resources often maintain and publish price reports, forest industry directories and summaries of market activities. Private forestry consultants and forest industry analysts also maintain websites with free, summary information and white papers.

Books: basic, introductory references can answer 80% of the day-to-day forest management questions, and even provide specifics on timber contracts and forest management plan. See "References and Recommended Resources" at the back of this book for suggestions.

Aunt Fanny Discusses Communication and Managing Risk

"Nephew, you've been in this forestry business for a while, right?" asked Aunt Fanny.

Oh, boy. The question triggered that tingling sensation on the back of my neck when the cards in the deck started turning against me. "Yes?" I said, hesitating.

Aunt Fanny laughed. She recognized the look on my face and put her hand on my arm to reassure me. "If I hire someone, or go to a doctor, or talk to a lawyer or see my mechanic...shoot, any 'professional' doing a job has a responsibility to communicate what they're doing and how it affects me."

"Amen," I said. "If you're my client and you want to know something, you deserve an explanation."

"Nephew," Aunt Fanny said, hands back on the hips of her camouflage jumpsuit. "Tell me more about your most successful clients. How do they communicate with their foresters? How do they manage the work? How do they manage risk?"

I looked into the woods and took in a deep breath through my nose. A whiff of honeysuckle scented the air. Two squirrels scampered off into the brush.

"Aunt Fanny, in my experience, successful forest owners do two things consistently and they do them well," I said. "First, they hire qualified professionals at the right price. And second, they manage the work they do with these professionals to get the services that they paid for."

Aunt Fanny looked at me and smiled. "Well said, Nephew."

"In forestry, our risks are two fold," I said. "First, we often don't know in the near term if a mistake has been made. Plant a tree incorrectly? Fail to fertilize properly? We may not know for years. Second, if a mistake is made, it compounds because we've lost value and opportunity over time."

"Exactly, this is what I'm worried about," said Aunt Fanny. "Dependence on others."

"I understand. And these other professionals include not just the forestry consultants and loggers, but the non-forestry service providers, too, such as lawyers and accountants," I said.

"And bankers," said Aunt Fanny.

"Yes, Ma'am," I said.

"Nephew, communication is a funny thing," said Aunt Fanny. **"Someone who talks a little and someone who talks a lot may both be telling you nothing."**

"Time for a story?" I asked.

"Absolutely!"

"Several years ago, a forest owner several counties away hired a consultant to manage a marked timber sale. The consultant marked the trees on his client's land that were for sale with blue paint. They conducted a successful bid sale with multiple potential buyers. The successful buyer hired a logger. The logger moved his crew and equipment onto the property and put a new hire into the cut down machine."

"I'm not liking where this is going," said Aunt Fanny, squinting her eyes in a pained expression and putting her hands up near her ears.

I continued. "This well-intentioned, young man climbed into that cut down machine and started skipping the blue-marked trees to cut down the unmarked ones."

"He didn't know," said Aunt Fanny, shaking her head.

"Nope, no one had walked him through the process. Classic failure to communicate," I said. "And not only were the wrong trees on the ground, but the landowner had to stare at a bunch of trees with blue paint on them for years."

The breeze picked up bringing back the honeysuckle scent. "A lot of the risk in forestry comes from miscommunication," I said. "You gotta confirm that the people you're working with know what they're doing, and you gotta stay in touch with them."

"I hear you, Nephew," said Aunt Fanny.

Aunt Fanny Prepares to Hire Forestry Professionals

Aunt Fanny crossed her arms across the front of her camouflage jumpsuit. "Nephew, tell me some war stories. What kinds of mistakes do forest owners make?"

"They don't hire me?" I said. We both laughed.

"Okay, smarty-pants, other than the obvious," said Aunt Fanny. She pulled out her black-and-white marbled composition notebook and Cross pen. "Ready when you are."

"Let's begin with the end in mind here," I said. "Our goal, first and foremost, is to hire folks who do what they say they are going to do when they say they are going to do it."

"Say that ten times fast," said Aunt Fanny, head down while writing in her notebook.

"Also, just because someone is nice does not mean they're trustworthy or competent," I said. "Forest owners make mistakes when they hire and, when necessary, fail to fire contractors who don't do what they agreed to do."

Aunt Fanny stopped writing and looked up at me. "Sounds like the voice of experience," she said. "You've got a few scars here."

"It's true," I said. "Most loggers and forestry consultants are true professionals. The good ones, those with whom we build strong working and personal relationships, are technically competent, have strong references, and communicate well."

"So what's the problem?" asked Aunt Fanny.

"Well some forest owners don't take the time to really evaluate and check out the folks they are hiring," I said. "In many cases, it's because they don't know how or they rely on their gut or they're too trusting."

"For example?" asked Aunt Fanny.

"For example, hiring a logger because you know his second cousin may not be best for your forest."

"Makes sense," said Aunt Fanny. "So what do you suggest?"

"Are you asking for my four step approach to hiring?"

"Yes, sir, Nephew sir," said Aunt Fanny, straightening up.

> **SIDEBAR: Four steps to evaluate and hire forestry professionals.**
>
> To systematically evaluate and select supporting professionals, consider the following four-step approach:
>
> *1. Write an interview guide*: an interview guide prepares you and lets candidates know that you care, so they should be prepared, too, when working with you in the future. A guide helps you compare candidates with a common set of questions. Finally, an interview guide protects you. "Well, it says right here in my notes from our interview that this is how you charge...." It also protects the service provider. Professional, well-prepared service providers like organized clients.
>
> *2. Do research*: search the Internet. Visit websites. Call other forest owners, extension foresters and state agencies for background information.
>
> *3. Check references*: call them. Understand EXACTLY why someone provided a positive referral.
>
> *4. Get it in writing*: NEVER agree to forestry work without a contract. And know what you're signing.
>
> Note: sample contracts are available from sources such as the Georgia Forestry Commission's website at www.gatrees.org. Go to "Forest Management" in the menu.

"First, write an interview guide," I said. "A simple list of questions helps prepare you. It organizes your thoughts and lets you compare candidates. It eliminates the problem of forgetting what questions you wished you had asked."

"Makes sense," said Aunt Fanny, writing in her notebook.

"Second, do your research," I said. "Research is like doing your reading before a lecture in school. If you do it, you will understand more and know what to look for during the interview. Call people. Go to the library. Search the Internet. Read."

"Okay," said Aunt Fanny.

"Third, after the interview, and assuming you're still interested in this person, check references," I said. "Visit the jobs they worked on. At the end of the day, success in forestry is about referrals and repeat business. So find out why other folks worked with them."

"Mmmmmm," said Aunt Fanny, nodding her head while writing.

"Finally, once you decide to move forward, get everything in writing," I said.

"Good stuff," said Aunt Fanny.

"But it doesn't end there," I said. "**Once you sign a contract, the real work begins**. You still need to manage the relationship with your contractors."

"What do you mean specifically, Nephew?" asked Aunt Fanny.

"Check the work," I said. "Dad always said you show what's important by how you spend your time, so get out there and check the work. Ask questions. And get answers. Listen and confirm that you understand, that they answered your questions. Your logger and forestry consultant will know you care if you walk the forest and check the work. You'll get a better result. If the work is not getting done correctly, ask to get it fixed. I do my best to be nice to people, but tough on issues that matter to my clients. If the work is still not getting done per the contract, make a change."

"Good advice," said Aunt Fanny.

"And write letters," I said. "Follow up in writing, even in an email, after meeting with people and agreeing to next steps. Write thank you notes for work well done or helpful referrals."

"Nephew, you're a regular Dear Abby," said Aunt Fanny, smiling.

SIDEBAR: Questions to include in an interview guide

What types of questions should forest owners include in an interview guide when meeting forestry service providers?

Background & experience: ask about education, how long they have been in business, and where they performed most of their work. One red flag: service providers who relocated their businesses and services frequently. As my Dad taught me years ago, "Ask yourself, 'are they running from something?'"

Training & certification: good loggers participate in their state and association training programs, such as Master Timber Harvester in Georgia and New York Logger Training in New York or Confirm the registration and certification of forestry consultants, CPAs, and attorneys.

Approach to the job: ask, "How would you approach this work? Can you walk me through this?" Then ask yourself, "Are they organized? Clear? Are they answering my questions?"

Communication: how do they stay in touch with clients? How can you reach them? With so many options – phones, email, texting, smoke signals – it helps to specify how communication will take place.

Insurance & liability: confirm they have the required coverage and get the documentation to prove it. If they are unwilling to provide a copy of insurance certificates, the interview is over. This risk is entirely manageable.

Fees & expenses: how much do these services cost? Who pays the expenses? Understand how this firm makes money. For example, if you are negotiating with a logger, understand who is actually buying the timber. The mill? The logger? Awareness of the relationships helps avoid future conflicts.

References: ask for and get names and contact information, including their relationships. Are they former clients? His Mom? Then call them.

Part III: Aunt Fanny Considers Another Timberland Investment

Aunt Fanny Discusses Timberland Returns

Aunt Fanny opened her black-and-white marbled composition notebook and flipped a few pages. Then she closed the book, put it under her arm and pulled out her Hewlett Packard calculator. She spoke while punching numbers into the HP.

"Know what you learn in banking? Nobody likes to lose money," said Aunt Fanny. "However, I also learned that investors have short memories at times. Folks simply forget that recessions happen every decade or so. At least. Markets go up and markets go down. Just part of the deal."

Before retiring, Aunt Fanny managed a group of bank branches in middle Georgia. She had worked her way up from secretary to regional vice president.

"Nephew, you've taught me a lot about my forest and how it can make me money. I see the cash flows. And investing more in timber sounds good. But I'm not sure the returns are there."

Aunt Fanny had shared her wisdom and experiences with me over the years. I remember her telling me once, years ago, while helping me with my math homework, "Numbers don't lie. People do."

Aunt Fanny continued clicking away on her calculator. A woodpecker in a nearby ash tree stopped poking for grubs and turned to watch. Aunt Fanny looked up; the woodpecker bobbed its head and flew off. I waited.

Aunt Fanny turned to me. "Alright, Nephew. Dazzle me."

"If you want to buy more timberland, **your returns depend largely on three things. One, what you pay for the forestland. Two, how long you stay invested. And three, how much you pay in fees to manage the forest.**"

Aunt Fanny nodded. "My valuation, my time horizon and my expenses."

"Right," I said. "These three largely determine your results. This is as true for the individual investor as it is for the largest pension fund."

"Nephew, are you oversimplifying this for me?"

"No, Ma'am. But I'm careful not to confuse simple with easy," I said. "We don't earn bonus points in forestry by making it complicated."

"There is no premium for complexity," said Aunt Fanny, nodding her head.

"Yep. That's what Dad always said," I said. "Nobody cares about the sophistication of your growth models or your Ivy League degree if the investments lose money. Simple, well-executed forest investment strategies and management plans keep the cow out of the ditch and on the road."

"Amen, Nephew."

We both looked into the forest towards the sounds of the woodpecker knocking about again.

"So what's the hard part?" asked Aunt Fanny.

"Patience," I said. "The hardest part is taking the time to get familiar with the local market to properly find and evaluate investment opportunities."

The woodpecker moved back to the favored ash tree.

"And," I added, "When the numbers look good, move fast."

Aunt Fanny Analyzes Her Timber Market

"Nephew, do you know Abe Phroman?" asked Aunt Fanny, looking out into the woods.

"Yes, he's the Sausage King of Chicago," I said.

"What?" said Aunt Fanny, scrunching her face like a Muppet. Apparently, she had not seen "Ferris Bueller's Day Off."

"Sorry," I said. "Old movie reference." I cleared my throat. "You mean your neighbor?"

"Exactly," said Aunt Fanny. "I suppose you already knew that Mr. Phroman is interested in selling some timberland."

"You mean the 184 acres of loblolly pine adjacent to your property to the north along the county road?" I said. "Yes, I had heard something about that."

"Well, I was thinking about thinking about making an offer," said Aunt Fanny.

I hesitated. "Did you just say what I think you said?"

"Yes," said Aunt Fanny. "I was thinking about whether or not to entertain this idea seriously. So how should I think about this?"

"Time for me to play professor again," I said.

"Okay," said Aunt Fanny, opening her composition notebook. "But be gentle. I'm not taking any quizzes."

"Overall, the recipe for assessing a potential timberland investment is straightforward," I said. "And it starts with understanding the local market for wood. Timber markets are uniquely local."

"What do you mean 'uniquely local'?" asked Aunt Fanny, making quotes in the air with the hand holding her pen. The other hand kept the notebook open.

"It means the same timberland property in two different markets will have two different values," I said. "You can have the finest timber in the world, but if you're not close enough to mills that can buy your trees and turn them into something more valuable such as lumber or paper, your trees, from an economic and investment standpoint, have little value."

"Well that's nice to hear," said Aunt Fanny, frowning behind her aviator sunglasses.

"In this case, since Mr. Phroman's property adjoins yours, we already know something about the local market," I said. "It's in your forest management plan."

Aunt Fanny reached to a side pocket in her camouflage jumpsuit and pulled out a folded sheaf of papers. She flipped several pages and started to read, "Local timber markets within 100 road miles include seven pine sawmills, two pine plywood plants, one pole plant, four hardwood grade mills, two pulp mills and four chip mills."

"So that gives us a starting point," I said. "Now we'd need to confirm that those mills are open and interested in the kind of timber we'd be selling from Mr. Phroman's land."

"Makes sense," said Aunt Fanny.

"Next, we would look closely at any data Mr. Phroman shares about his forest and we'd ask questions," I said. "Remember, forestry has a somewhat bizarre relationship with data. Everything is a sample. A forest cruise is a sample of what's out there. Any timber price data is based on a sample of what's going on in the market."

"Would we do our own cruise to check the forest?" asked Aunt Fanny.

"There's a good chance we would," I said. "Because, in the end, we want to know what's knowable. This helps us minimize any risks. We want to know, as best as possible, what we're buying and, to the extent possible, the potential revenues and property taxes and management costs."

"Whew," said Aunt Fanny.

"In the end, we want to understand the individual property and the local timber market," I said. "Timberland values depend on the local wood basin and the value of the forest growing on the properties."

"Well, I guess we should go talk to Mr. Phroman," said Aunt Fanny. "Life moves pretty fast. If we don't stop talking and look around, we could miss an opportunity."

Aunt Fanny Asks About Timber Prices, Again

Aunt Fanny flipped through the figures and tables in the forestry newsletter and asked, "When will the timber market return to normal?"

"Aunt Fanny, there is no such thing as a normal forest or a normal timber market," I said. "According to one of my forestry professors, 'both are pedagogical fictions.'"

"What the heck does that mean?" asked Aunt Fanny.

"I asked him the same thing. He said, 'it means we made them up to teach clueless undergraduates.'"

"Oh. Sounds honest enough." Aunt Fanny looked up into the trees. "So there's no 'normal' market?"

"All my clients ask me the same thing," I said. "They ask, 'How much longer must we wait for prices to return to normal?' In practice, who knows?"

"Nephew, you speak truth. When I worked at the bank, it seemed the economy or money market was always booming or busting. Sliding or skidding."

"Yes, Ma'am."

"Philosophize a bit, Nephew," said Aunt Fanny. "I invite you to the soap box."

I put my fists on my hips and pretended to step up onto a platform. "**Timber prices have limits**. They operate in a box. They can only go so low, or landowners, like yourself, lose money and find tree planting pointless. And prices can only go so high, or mills have to pay too much for the logs and end up losing money."

"Nephew, you're talking real world language. This sounds like the price of money."

I looked at Aunt Fanny and raised an eyebrow.

"When I managed those banks, we always talked about the price of money. That was our product. We bought money at one price, through offering savings accounts, and sold money at another price, through offering loans."

"Okay, that makes sense."

"The difference between what we paid in interest to savers and what we received in interest from borrows was our revenue."

"How much of that was profit?" I asked.

"Whatever was left over after we covered our overhead. Salaries. Rent. Free toasters."

I nodded like I knew what she was talking about.

"When you talked about timber prices operating in a box, it was the same with money. Pay too little in interest, and no one will open a savings account. Charge too much in interest, and no one will take a loan," said Aunt Fanny.

"Right," I said. "Though selling timber is a bit unique."

"How so?" asked Aunt Fanny.

"Compare it to selling other commodities. While oil and corn are sold in global and national markets, timber is sold 'on the stump' in your forest," I said, making quotes in the air with my hands.

"So how would that affect me?" asked Aunt Fanny.

"It means that the specific quality of your trees and the mileage to the mill from your forest affect what a timber buyer could pay," I said. "And that's in addition to the demand for and prices of products sold by the mills themselves, like lumber and pulp."

"It's a balancing act in a competitive marketplace."

Aunt Fanny Asks About Forestland Appreciation

Aunt Fanny put the HP calculator back in the pocket of her camouflage jumpsuit. She looked down and around at the ground covered in leaves, needles and twigs. Then, she turned to me and asked, "Nephew, what makes my forestland more valuable? What causes the land to appreciate?"

I nodded and took a deep breath. "There's a lot going on here. I'll do my best to share what I know."

"I'd expect nothing less, young man," said Aunt Fanny, pulling out her Cross pen and marbled composition notebook.

"To start, **your forest doesn't grow in a vacuum**. We grow the trees with certain markets in mind. The mills we sell wood to today will probably be the same mills we sell logs to in ten years," I said.

Aunt Fanny nodded while making a brief note in her notebook.

I continued, "But the land is subject to other economic…forces. And these forces can create value."

"Keep it grounded, Nephew. You sound like Yoda. What forces?"

"I think about two things: people and alternative uses."

"Continue, young Jedi."

"Well, people put pressure on the land. Wherever you have a lot of people, you have a lot of homebuilding, stores, schools and roads. The value of the land goes up and, in a way, it becomes too 'valuable' for growing trees."

"I've seen this happen. When I was a girl, they built the highway through our county. Forests and small farms became the four-lane and a series of towns," said Aunt Fanny.

"Yes, Ma'am. The US Forest Service published an article that describes this relationship between population density and land values. Once you have more than 150 people per square mile, on average, land values start climbing and putting pressure on forests."

"Nephew, you also mentioned alternative uses. This sounds like the same thing to me," said Aunt Fanny.

"It's related," I said. "Basically, I think about it more from the perspective of my clients. They'll ask, 'should I plant trees or row crops?'"

"We used to deal with similar questions when I worked at the bank," said Aunt Fanny, thinking back to her days as a regional vice president. "We would talk about the best use of our capital, our funds."

"Yes, Ma'am. Opportunity cost."

"Exactly," said Aunt Fanny. "**We create wealth wherever we focus capital and effort**. When we financed a building, some thought the money disappeared. Did it? No! We paid dozens or hundreds of people, from construction workers to surveyors to lawyers to electricians and plumbers and painters."

"And the land appreciates," I said.

"Exactly," said Aunt Fanny.

"And it also increases the cost of owning the land," I said.

"Right. Property taxes and insurance, for example," said Aunt Fanny. "It's a circle."

"More people or more valuable uses of the land, from an income standpoint, put pressure on the forest. And this pushes forestland values up."

Aunt Fanny Decides to Value a Forest

I drove out through the old swing gate at the front of the woods road and stepped out of the truck to close the gate and lock it. Aunt Fanny opened the passenger side door and climbed down from the seat. She adjusted the aviator sunglasses on her nose.

"Nephew, do we really need to lock that gate?" asked Aunt Fanny.

"Well, a wise woman once told me that we don't live in Mayberry."

Aunt Fanny laughed. "That's true, Nephew. At the bank, I kept a fifth of Wild Turkey in my desk for friends and a .38 Special for special situations."

"You ever use it?" I asked.

"Every week," said Aunt Fanny, pausing. "What's the point of having bourbon nearby if you aren't going to drink it?"

"Ba dum chhh." I whispered, pantomiming a drummer's rim shot at a comedy club. We smiled.

Aunt Fanny looked down the county road towards her neighbor's forest. "Nephew, I'd like to make an offer to Mr. Phroman on his forest," she said. "But first, I'd like you to talk me out of it."

"Okay, this should be fun," I said. "First, remember that **trees don't grow to the sky.**"

"What do you mean by that?" asked Aunt Fanny

"A solid, successful timberland investment has a clear management plan, implemented well and a sound and sensible acquisition price," I said. "If we mess up the valuation, it's hard to make up that kind of ground with a forest."

"I get it. We need to buy it right," said Aunt Fanny.

"Also, the forest, especially a smaller property, may generate negative cash flows for a while," I said.

"Nephew, why would I keep an investment with negative cash flows?"

"Over the long haul, you wouldn't," I said. "Timber properties create value through cash flows."

"Right," replied Aunt Fanny.

"But buying a young forest may require investment or waiting on future harvests and cash flows," I said. "And buying a mid-term forest may generate modest cash flows from thinnings. While you should expect positive returns, the source and timing of those returns, and the nature of the cash flows, will differ."

"You managing my expectations?" asked Aunt Fanny, raising an eyebrow in my direction.

"Yes, Ma'am, I am," I said. "And there's more to think about. How much will it cost to own and manage the property? Are the roads any good, or will we need to spend money there? Do we have reasonable access to all of the acres, or do we need easements from other neighboring landowners? Is there clear title to the land and are the boundaries well marked? Does the property have special features, like ponds, that make the property more or less valuable to you or potential buyers in the future?"

"Okay, now you're making me think twice again," said Aunt Fanny.

"You asked me to talk you out of it," I said. "At the end of the day, we just want to do our homework and make a fair offer that meets your objectives and reflects the local markets."

"Yes, that's right," said Aunt Fanny.

"And if we buy the forest right, you'll have a solid asset in your portfolio," I said.

"Well let's get valuing then, Nephew!"

Conclusion

Aunt Fanny's Ode to Forest Ownership

I woke up, on schedule, at 4:14 in the morning, rolled over and switched off the alarm before it chimed. At 4:15, the phone buzzed.

"Good morning, Nephew!" said Aunt Fanny. "You up?"

"Yes, Ma'am," I said, swinging my legs over the side of the bed and slipping my feet into the cool fleece inside the moccasins on the floor.

"You pick up your mail yesterday?" asked Aunt Fanny.

"No, Ma'am," I responded while standing up.

"Didn't think so," said Aunt Fanny. "I was expecting a call that didn't come." Then she hung up.

Curious, I pulled on a pair of jeans and sweatshirt to walk outside. Inside the mailbox, I found a thermos-sized cardboard box and a plain white envelope addressed to me.

# # #

Back in the house, I started the coffee pot and sat down at the kitchen table with the box and envelope. Inside the envelope was a folded sheet of paper with a yellow sticky note attached. The sticky note included a message in Aunt Fanny's clear handwriting. It said:

> *Nephew,*
>
> *Thank you for everything you taught me. After buying Mr. Phroman's property, I felt inspired to put thoughts on paper. Behold my 'Ode to Forest Ownership!'*
>
> *Look forward to your thoughts.*
>
> *Love,*
>
> *Aunt Fanny*
>
> *P.S. Enjoy the treats!*

Inside the box, I found a bottle of Wild Turkey bourbon, a silver Cross pen with my name engraved on the side and a blue roll of mint Mentos. Smiling, I unfolded the sheet of paper and read.

Ode to Forest Ownership

The forest will grow with or without a hand,
Yet ownership offers a way to shape stands.
To keep your forest productive and healthy,
Consider this ode to also grow wealthy.

First choose what you want from your acres of woods,
Ask, "Do I prize hikes, hunts or tree livelihoods?"
If financial returns and cash top the list,
Take time to know more so key steps are not missed.

Next measure your forest to know what you've got,
Count trees with a cruise in a clear grid of plots.
This also may give you a chance to roam free,
Walk through your stands; learn the rustle of trees.

Third take stock of your stands in light of your goals,
Write a management plan with timing and roles.
One gets no results with a plan on the shelf,
Implement with a team or go do it yourself.

Keep risks in perspective, they're neither mean nor nice,
Take real care when you hire or go seeking advice.
A clean truck and a smile do not tell you enough,
Pick those who do what they say, on time, without guff.

Successful wood owners do more than love trees,
They make choices, have plans, know good advice isn't free.
Go get smart on your market, hire folks that are true,
So that your forest will grow, prosper, and thrill you.

Checklists

These checklists provide a working set of priorities for minimizing errors, mitigating risks and maximizing returns from potential timberland investments. Consider them a starting point for thinking through the valuations and opportunities of candidate properties.

Investing in Timberland

Investing in and managing timberland requires discipline, patience and a sharp pencil. Big jobs, done well, take time. And successful timberland investing and management take time. How can any forester plant and manage well a forest quickly? How can we develop strong relationships with local markets without time? How can we expect a deep understanding of how and why our forest prospered or failed, and how to deal with the small, unavoidable challenges of owning and analyzing our forest investments in turbulent environments?

1. <u>Specify objectives</u>. This is harder than it sounds. Goals must be simple, clearly defined and prioritized. Forest investing awards no bonus points for degrees of difficulty. Forest investments are attractive because they simply (not 'easily') provide a long-term option to protect, hold and increase wealth.
2. <u>Question forest data and financial analysis</u>. In forestry, everything is a sample. A forest cruise is a sample of the standing inventory. Timber pricing services report a sample of prices from market transactions. Ask questions about the data and the assumptions in any price forecasts and financial analysis. How do the results square with history, logic, market tolerances and the time/space continuum as you understand it?
3. <u>Think like a business owner</u> before making any investment. Probe the business strategy; does the investment "make sense"? Talk through the plan in detail before moving forward. Understand your options for recovering your

capital if the investment does not go as planned. Save gambling for the riverboat.
4. <u>Understand the local wood market</u> when reviewing a timberland property. Timber markets are uniquely local. The same property in two different baskets will have two different values. Understand why. This goes beyond knowing the mills to which you might sell logs. Know in advance how you or your manager will access these markets. Will you work through a forestry consultant? If so, who? How will you manage local relationships?
5. <u>Understand the 'true' risks</u> and protect accordingly. Have a risk management plan and reasonable levels of insurance as required by law and helpful to long-term security. Timberland novices ask about fire, bugs, disease and hurricanes. Forest investment professionals can put these risks into perspective. They will tell you to worry more about markets, communicate with your forest manager and properly insure against landowner liabilities.
6. <u>Understand taxes and tax exposures.</u> You can make a lot of money and lose a lot of money based on what you (and your accountant) know or don't know about timber taxes.
7. <u>Watch expenses</u>. Expenses have a way of growing in proportion with or beyond our incomes. Don't confuse "necessity" with "desire." Make a budget and manage against it. Understand your cash flows, management fees and exactly who pays for what.

In the end, **be brave and face facts**. Will this timberland investment *really* generate 7% annual returns? How? Under what conditions? The investing process includes both the asking of questions and the getting of answers. These two different tasks help clarify assumptions, confirm competence and increase the likelihood of investment success.

Basic Steps for Valuing a Forest

The basic process for valuing timberlands requires collecting forest and market data, modeling forest growth and yields, and conducting financial analysis of estimated future cash flows. The list below includes basic steps in the process.

1. <u>Characterize the current forest</u>. Quantify (cruise) the current volume and inventory by product and specie. Capture the information required to generate a growth and yield model, such as site index, acres, and how many of these acres are operable. While doing this, capture supplementary information related to markets, hauling distances and logging costs that will further support an understanding of the true market values and operating costs.
2. <u>Generate a growth and yield model of the forest</u>. Also called a "forest estate model", this projects the harvest volumes (yields) by product and year over the investment period. Often this requires the support of a forestry consultant or software to model the forest forward. Yield refers to what the forest 'yields' in saleable timber products... forest yield and stumpage prices determine the revenue from selling timber.
3. <u>Build a "discounted cash flow" (DCF) model to estimate forest value</u>. This takes the future cash flows and nets the revenues against costs. Harvest revenues will include assumptions related to future timber prices and alternate income sources such as hunting leases. Costs will include silvicultural expenses, management fees, property taxes, and other items. The DCF model also requires the selection of an appropriate discount rate, which may correspond to your required rate of return or cost of capital.
4. <u>Identify the optimum economic rotation for the forest</u>. Using the DCF model, we can identify the rotation age that maximizes the bare land value (BLV). This also helps determine the optimal forest management strategy for the forest.
5. <u>Estimate the net present value (NPV) based on the investment horizon</u>. This will require a terminal value for exiting the investment that would be based on the expected

forest inventory at the end of the analysis or investment period. The NPV helps us zero in an offer price for the property.
6. <u>Conduct a sensitivity analysis</u>. Key assumptions to test include the discount rate, harvest yields, stumpage forecasts and cost assumptions. Ask "where are the key risks and how should our offer give us an appropriate margin for error?"

Glossary

Acre   area of land containing 43,560 square feet, or approximately equal to a square with sides of just over 208 feet each

Bare land value (BLV)   present net worth of bare forestland for timber production estimated over a perpetual series of rotations; also referred to as land expectation value (LEV) or soil expectation value (SEV)

Bueller, Ferris   lead character, played by Matthew Broderick, in the 1986 film "Ferris Bueller's Day Off", written and directed by John Hughes. In one scene, Bueller pretends to be Abe Froman, the "Sausage King of Chicago," to secure a table at a fancy restaurant.

Capital   an asset that can be invested and used to generate income or grow wealth

Cash flow   measure of investment or firm liquidity; comprised of net income plus non-cash expenditures (such as amortization, depletion and depreciation); notable saying: "cash is king"

Chip-n-saw   timber product from mid-sized trees that makes small dimension lumber and chips for fuel or paper production. The name comes from the manufacturing process for this log, where the outer slabs are chipped while the center is sawed into lumber.

Cominant trees   trees with crowns that receive full sunlight from above and, compared to dominant trees, relatively little from the sides

Cost of capital   rate of interest a firm pays to secure financing (debt or equity) from investors buying the firm's stock or bonds

Crop tree   tree selected during a thinning to remain as part of the future stand and final harvest; crop trees chosen by having the greatest potential growth in value over time

Cruise   systematic survey of a forest to estimate the number, size, value and volume of the trees by specie and product on the land; also used to identify key features and conditions relevant to forest management activities

Diameter at breast height (DBH)   tree diameter measured at 4.5 feet off the average ground level at the base of the tree

Discount rate   interest rate used to discount future cash flows; rate of return required to justify investment

Dominant trees   trees with crowns that receive full sunlight from above and partly from the side; typically these trees are larger than the average trees in the stand.

Forest   area of land covered mostly with trees and other organisms associated with trees, soil, water, etc

Growth and yield model   quantitative approach to projecting the increase of (growth) and wood volume available from (yield) a forest given a certain management plan; models typically rely on statistical analysis to capture key biologic relationships.

Harmon, Mark   American actor; stars as a former Marine turned NCIS Special Agent Leroy Jethro Gibbs in the CBS television series, *NCIS*. Harmon was UCLA's starting quarterback in 1972 and 1973; his father, Tom, won the Heisman Trophy.

Inflation   the general increase in prices and wages over time and the associated (and unpleasant) reduction in the buying power of money

Internal rate of return (IRR)   discount rate that makes the NPV of a potential investment equal to zero

Land expectation value (LEV)   see "Bare land value"

Mayberry   fictional North Carolina town that served as the setting for the 1960s television sitcom "The Andy Griffith Show." Often used to reference an ideal, small town.

Mentos   one of my favorite candies; chewy mints with a slight, crunchy crust; originally produced in The Netherlands in the 1940s, they are now also available in fruity flavors (which are favorites of my daughters)

Muppet   puppet characters created by Jim Henson in 1955; featured in the television show *The Muppet Show* and other Disney movies and productions. Some of the most famous characters include Kermit the Frog and Miss Piggy.

Net present value (NPV)   present value of future revenues minus present value of future costs

Opportunity cost   opportunity lost to invest in something other than your chosen investment; rate of return on the best alternative investment that is not chosen

Padawan   in the Star Wars movies, a "Padawan" refers to a Jedi apprentice who had started their one-on-one training with a Jedi Knight or Jedi Master

Plywood   flat wood panels made from compressing and gluing together a number of thin sheets of wood (veneers); the veneers come from "peeling" on a lathe or slicing high quality, larger sawtimber.

Pre-merchantable timber   also called "premerch"; refers to commercial species that are too young or small for sale to wood-using mills

Present value   cash value today of future cash flows

Pulpwood   timber product from smaller sized and low quality trees used for fuel or paper production

Real assets (property)   assets such as forests, buildings and other real estate, bridges and other infrastructure that would be tough to move

Rotation   length of time between planting and harvesting an even-aged stand of trees

Sawmill   manufacturing facility that converts sawtimber or chip-n-saw logs into lumber

Sawtimber   timber product from larger trees (larger than chip-n-saw) of good quality used to make lumber.

Silviculture   theory and practice of establishing (planting) and managing stands of trees to meet specific objectives; objectives typically relate to forest health, productivity, aesthetics, financial performance or wildlife.

Site index   measure used to indicate potential tree growth at a specific location or "site" based on height; the number used refers to the average height of the dominant and codominant trees at a reference age of 25, 50 or 100 years, depending on the specie and geographic region.

Soil expectation value (SEV)   see "Bare land value"

Stumpage   value of standing trees "on the stump"; price of the trees that a landowner receives from a timber sale

Thinning   type of partial forest harvest in which only selected trees are removed from the stand to provide room and resources for the future growth of the remaining, highest potential trees

Timber   standing trees; see "stumpage"

Timberland forested land capable of growing a minimum of 20 cubic feet/acre/year; also known as commercial forestland (definition: U.S. Forest Service)

Yield total forest growth in volume over a period of time, net of mortality and unmerchantable (non commercial) trees

References and Recommended Resources

Clason, George. 2002. *The Richest Man in Babylon*. Signet. 144 pages.

Greene, J.L.; Siegel, W.C.; Hoover, W.L.; Koontz, M. 2012. *Forest landowners' guide to the Federal income tax*. Agriculture Handbook 731. Washington, DC: U.S. Department of Agriculture.

Hardin, Philip A. (editor). 2009. *Woodlands Management Course: A Guide to Improving Our Forests*, The Forest Landowner Foundation, Atlanta, Georgia, 282 pages.

McEvoy, Thom J. 2005. *Owning and Managing Forests: A Guide to Legal, Financial and Practical Matters*, Island Press, Washington, 300 pages.

Mendell, Brooks C. 2014. *Forest Finance Simplified, 5th Edition*. Forisk Press, 101 pages.

Mendell, Brooks C. 2009. Strategies for managing risk to meet forest landowner objectives, *Forest Landowner*, May/June, p. 26-28.

Mendell, Brooks C. 2006. *Loving Trees is Not Enough: Communication Skills for Natural Resource Professionals*, Aventine Press. 114 pages.

Mendell, Brooks C. 2005. Risk and liability concerns facing forest landowners. *Forest Landowner*, March/April, 64(2):12-13.

Price, Terry. 2008. *Forest Health Guide for Georgia, 3rd Edition*. Georgia Forestry Commission, 158 pages. Available at http://www.forestpests.org/gfcbook/FHG050108.pdf

Stephens, Rockwell R. 1974. *One Man's Forest: Managing Your Woodlot for Pleasure and Profit*, The Stephen Greene Press, Brattleboro, Vermont, 159 pages.

U.S. Forest Service Cooperative Forestry. Go to: www.fs.fed.us/spf/coop/

Wang, Linda. 2014. Tax tips for forest landowners. USDA Forest Service. Available at www.timbertax.org, 2 pages.

Wear, David N. and David H. Newman. 2004. The speculative shadow over timberland values in the U.S. South. *Journal of Forestry*, 102(8): 25-31. Available from the USDA Forest Service website at http://www.srs.fs.usda.gov/pubs/7730

Forestry and Forest Owner Associations by State

National
Forest Landowners Association (FLA)
- www.forestlandowners.com; 800-325-2954

National Alliance of Forest Owners (NAFO)
- www.nafoalliance.org; 202-747-0759

National Woodland Owners Association (NWOA)
- www.woodlandowners.org; 703-255-2700

Alabama
Alabama Forest Owners Association (AFOA)
- www.afoa.org; 205-987-8811

Alabama Forestry Association
- www.alaforestry.org; 334-265-8733

Alaska
Alaska Forest Association
- www.akforest.org; 907-225-6114

Arizona
Arizona State Forestry Division
- www.azsf.az.gov; 602-771-1400

Arkansas
Arkansas Forestry Association
- www.arkforests.org; 501-374-2441

California
Forest Landowners of California (FLC)
- www.forestlandowners.org; 877-326-3778

California Forestry Association
- www.calforests.org; 916-444-6592

Colorado
Colorado Forestry Association
- www.coloradoforestry.org; 970-531-9421

Connecticut
Eastern Connecticut Forest Landowners Association (ECFLA)
- www.ecfla.org; 860-774-5444

Connecticut Forest & Parks Association
- www.ctwoodlands.org; 860-346-8733

Delaware
Delaware Forestry Association
- www.delawareforest.com; 410896-9283

Florida
Florida Forestry Association
- www.floridaforest.org; 850-222-5646

Georgia
Georgia Forestry Association
- www.gfagrow.org; 478-992-8110

Hawaii
Hawaii Forest Industry Association
- www.hawaiiforest.org; 808-933-9411

Idaho
Idaho Forest Owners Association (IFOA)
- www.idahoforestowners.org

Idaho Forest Products Commission
- www.idahoforests.org; 208-334-3292

Illinois
Illinois Forestry Association
- www.ilforestry.org

Indiana
Indiana Forestry & Woodland Owners Association (IFWOA)
- www.ifwoa.org; 765-583-3501

Iowa
Iowa Woodland Owners Association (IWOA)
- www.iowawoodlandowners.org

Kansas
Kansas Forest Service
- www.kansasforests.org; 785-532-3300

Kentucky
Kentucky Woodland Owners Association (KWOA)
- www.kwoa.net; 606-876-3423

Kentucky Forest Industries Association
- www.kfia.org; 502-695-3979

Louisiana
Louisiana Forestry Association
- www.laforestry.com; 318-443-2558

Maine
Small Woodland Owners Association of Maine (SWOAM)
- www.swoam.org; 207-626-0005

Forest Society of Maine
- www.fsmaine.org; 207-945-9200

Maryland
Maryland Forests Association
- www.mdforests.org; 410-823-1789

Massachusetts
Massachusetts Forest Alliance
- www.massforests.org; 617-455-9918

Michigan
Michigan Forest Association
- www.michiganforests.org; 517-663-3423

Minnesota
Minnesota Forestry Association
- www.minnesotaforestry.org; 218-326-6486

Mississippi
Mississippi Forestry Association
- www.msforestry.net; 601-354-4936

Missouri
Missouri Forest Products Association
- www.moforest.org; 573-634-3252

Montana
Montana Forest Owners Association (MFOA)
- www.forestsmontana.com

Montana Wood Products Association
- www.montanaforests.com; 406-241-7047

Nebraska
Nebraska Forest Service
- www.nfs.unl.edu; 402-472-2944

Nevada
Nevada Division of Forestry
- www.forestry.nv.gov; 775-684-2500

New Hampshire
New Hampshire Timberland Owners Association (NHTOA)
- www.nhtoa.org; 603-224-9699

New Hampshire Division of Forests and Land
- www.nhdfl.org; 603-271-2214

New Jersey
New Jersey Forestry Association
- www.njforestry.org; 908-832-2400

New Mexico
New Mexico Forest Industry Association
- www.nmfia.org; 505-705-0166

New York
New York Forest Owners Association (NYFOA)
- www.nyfoa.org; 585-624-3385

Empire State Forest Products Association
- www.esfpa.org; 518-463-1297

North Carolina
NCWoodlands
- www.ncwoodlands.org; 919-787-1220

North Carolina Forestry Association
- www.ncforestry.org; 800-231-7723

North Dakota
North Dakota Forest Service
- www.ndsu.nodak.edu/forestservice; 701-228-5422

Ohio
Ohio Forestry Association
- www.ohioforest.org; 614-497-9580

Oklahoma
Oklahoma Woodland Owners Association

Oklahoma Forestry Association

Oklahoma Forestry Services
- www.forestry.ok.gov; 405-522-6158

Oregon
Oregon Small Woodlands Association (OSWA)
- www.oswa.org; 503-588-1813

Oregon Forest Industries Council
- www.ofic.com; 503-371-2942

Pennsylvania
Pennsylvania Woodland Owners Associations
- www.extension.psu.edu/natural-resources/forests/private/woodland-owners-associations; 800-235-9473

Pennsylvania Forestry Association
- www.paforestry.org; 800-835-8065

Rhode Island
Rhode Island Forest Conservators Organization
- www.rifco.org; 401-568-3421

South Carolina
South Carolina Forestry Association
- www.scforestry.org; 803-798-4170

South Dakota
Intermountain Forest Association
- www.intforest.org; 605-341-0875

Black Hills Forest Resource Association
- www.bhfra.org; 605-341-0875

Tennessee
Tennessee Woodland Owners Association

Tennessee Forestry Association
- www.tnforestry.com; 615-883-3832

Texas
Texas Forest Landowners Council
- www.texasforestry.org/programs/owners

Texas Forestry Association
- www.texasforestry.org; 936-632-8733

Utah
Utah Woodland Owners Council

Utah Division of Forestry
- www.ffsl.utah.gov/index.php/forestry; 801-538-5504

Vermont
Vermont Woodlands Association (VMA)
- www.vermontwoodlands.org; 802-747-7900

Vermont Forest Products Association
- www.vtfpa.org; 802-491-5688

Virginia
Virginia Forestry Association
- www.vaforestry.org; 804-278-8733

Washington
Washington Farm Forestry Association (WFFA)
- www.wafarmforestry.com; 360-388-7074

Washington Forest Protection Association
- www.wfpa.org; 360-352-1500

West Virginia
Woodland Owners of West Virginia

West Virginia Forestry Association
- www.wvfa.org; 304-372-1955

Wisconsin
Wisconsin Woodland Owners Association (WWOA)
- www.wisconsinwoodlands.org; 715-346-4798

Wisconsin County Forests Association
- www.wisconsincountyforests.com; 715-282-5951

Wyoming
Black Hills Forest Resource Association
- www.bhfra.org; 605-341-0875

About the Author

Dr. Brooks Mendell is President and Founder of Forisk Consulting. His experience includes roles in forestry operations with Weyerhaeuser, in forest industry consulting with Accenture, and in academia as a faculty member at the University of Georgia. An award-winning speaker, he has published articles and books on topics related to wood bioenergy, timber markets, timberland investments and REITs, forestry operations, and business communications. He earned B.S. and M.S. degrees at the Massachusetts Institute of Technology, an MBA at the University of California–Berkeley, and a Ph.D. in Forest Finance at the University of Georgia.

About Forisk Consulting

Forisk provides research and education in the forestry, timberland and wood bioenergy sectors. Forisk advises senior executives in areas such as business strategy, asset and market due diligence, and timber market and risk analysis. Forisk delivers products and services in the U.S. and internationally to corporations, government and educational institutions, not-for-profit organizations, small enterprises and private individuals and investors. Founded in 2004, Forisk has been a four-time "Bulldog 100 Fastest Growing Business."

Websites

- Forisk website, blog and store: www.forisk.com

The Forisk News

Forisk offers free email subscriptions to the **Forisk News**, which contains research summaries related to timberland investments and markets, forestry, and forest products. We publish the Forisk News four to six times per year. Sign up for our email distributions on the Forisk website at forisk.com or email Heather Clark directly at hclark@forisk.com.

Products and Books

We offer products that support our ongoing research associated with investments and timber prices in the timberland and wood-using sectors. These include the **Forisk Research Quarterly (*FRQ*)** and the **Timberland Owner List**. Detailed information can be found on Forisk's website.

In addition, the following books by Forisk authors are available:
- *Forest Finance Simplified, 5th Edition* by Brooks Mendell, published by Forisk Press in 2014.
- *Wood for Bioenergy: Forests as a Resource for Biomass and Biofuels* by Brooks Mendell and Amanda Lang, published by the Forest History Society in 2012.
- *Loving Trees is Not Enough: Communication Skills for Natural Resource Professionals* by Brooks Mendell, published by Aventine Press in 2006.

Forisk Continuing Education Program

Forisk offers specialized training for professionals and investors in the fields of forestry, bioenergy, and timberland and timber REIT investing. In addition to public short courses, Forisk provides internal Executive Education and Skill Development Workshops for organizations interested in customized courses.

Customized Presentations and Speeches

We offer educational and dynamic presentations related to forest finance, wood bioenergy, and timber markets. Workshops and speeches can be tailored and customized to cover "hot" issues for a wide range of professional audiences.